Utt
Beasts

The Bad Child's Book of Beasts

and

More Beasts (for worse children)

Verses by Hilaire Belloc

Pictures by Basil Temple Blackwood

THE BAD CHILD'S BOOK OF BEASTS

Verses by
H. BELLOC

Pictures by
B. T. B.

Child! do not throw this book about;
Refrain from the unholy pleasure
Of cutting all the pictures out!
Preserve it as your chiefest treasure.

Child, have you never heard it said
That you are heir to all the ages?
Why, then, your hands were never made
To tear these beautiful thick pages!

Your little hands were made to take
The better things and leave the worse ones.
They also may be used to shake
The Massive Paws of Elder Persons.

And when your prayers complete the day,
Darling, your little tiny hands
Were also made, I think, to pray
For men that lose their fairylands.

DEDICATION

To

Master EVELYN BELL
Of Oxford

Evelyn Bell,
I love you well.

INTRODUCTION

I CALL you bad, my little child,
Upon the title page,
Because a manner rude and wild
Is common at your age.

The Moral of this priceless work
(If rightly understood)
Will make you—from a little Turk—
Unnaturally good.

Do not as evil children do,
Who on the slightest grounds
Will imitate

the Kangaroo,
With wild unmeaning bounds.

Do not as children badly bred,
Who eat like little Hogs,
And when they have to go to bed
Will whine like Puppy Dogs:

Who take their manners from the Ape,
Their habits from the Bear,
Indulge the loud unseemly jape,
And never brush their hair.

But so control your actions that
Your friends may all repeat.

'This child is dainty as the Cat,
And as the Owl discreet.'

The Yak

As a friend to the children

commend me the Yak.

You will find it exactly the thing:

It will carry and fetch,

you can ride on its back,

Or lead it about

with a string.

The Tartar who dwells on the plains of
Thibet

(A desolate region of snow)

Has for centuries made it a nursery pet,

And surely the Tartar should know!

Then tell your papa where the Yak can be
got,

And if he is awfully rich

He will buy you the creature—

or else

he will *not*.

(I cannot be positive which.)

The Polar Bear

The Polar Bear is unaware

Of cold that cuts me through:
For why? He has a coat of hair.
I wish I had one too!

The Lion

The Lion, the Lion, he dwells in the waste,

He has a big head and a very small waist;

But his shoulders are stark, and his jaws
they are grim,

And a good little child will not play with
him.

The Tiger

The Tiger on the other hand,

is kittenish and mild,

He makes a pretty playfellow for any little child;

And mothers of large families (who claim to common sense)

Will find a Tiger well repay the trouble and expense.

The Dromedary

The Dromedary is a cheerful bird:

I cannot say the same about the Kurd.

The Whale

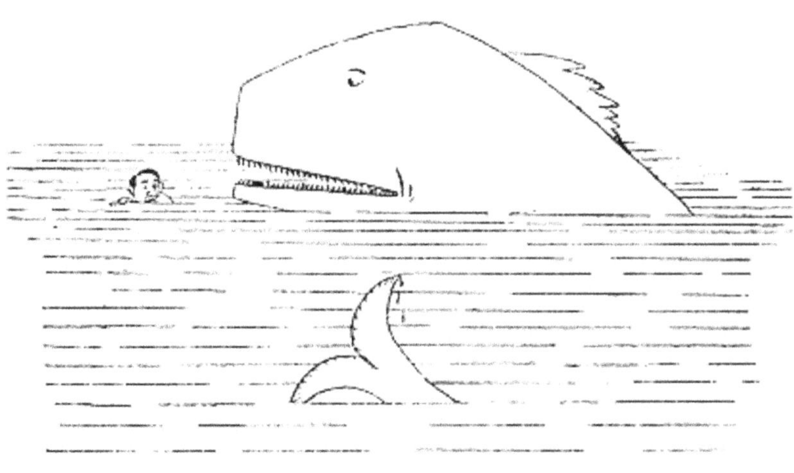

The Whale that wanders round the Pole

Is not

a table fish.

You cannot bake or boil him whole

Nor serve him in a dish;

But you may cut his blubber up

And melt it down for oil,

And so replace

the colza bean

(A product of the soil).

These facts should all be noted down
    And ruminated on,

By every boy in Oxford town
    Who wants to be a Don.

The Camel

"The Ship of the Desert."

The Hippopotamus

I shoot the Hippopotamus

with bullets made of platinum,

Because if I use leaden ones

his hide is sure to flatten 'em

The Dodo

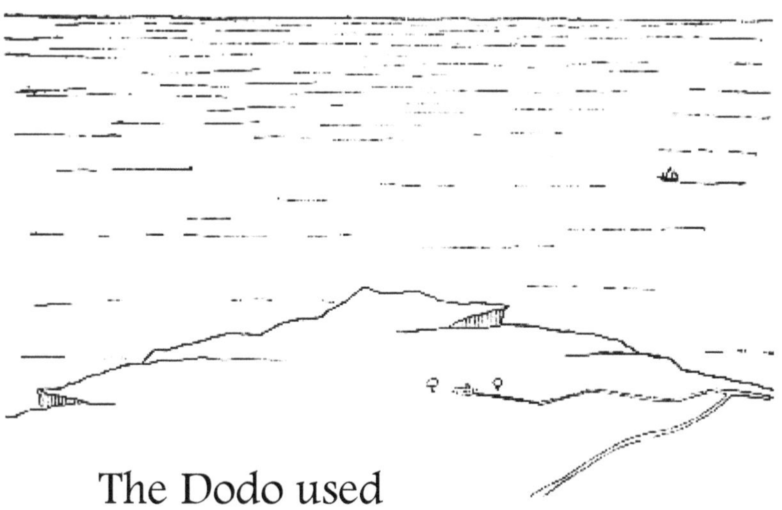

The Dodo used

to walk around,

And take the sun and air.

The sun yet warms his native ground—

The Dodo is not there!

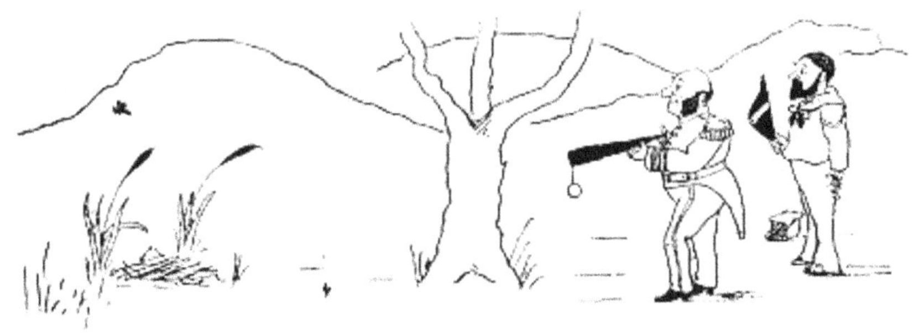

The voice which used to squawk and
squeak

Is now for ever dumb—

Yet may you see his bones and beak
All in the Mu-se-um.

The Marmozet

The species Man and Marmozet
Are intimately linked;

The Marmozet survives as yet,
But Men are all extinct.

The Camelopard

The Camelopard, it is said

By travellers (who never lie),

He cannot stretch out straight in bed
Because he is so high.
The clouds surround his lofty head,
His hornlets touch the sky.

How shall
I hunt this quadruped?
I cannot tell!
Not I!

(A picture of how people try
And fail to hit that head so high.)

I'll buy a little parachute
 (A common parachute with wings),
I'll fill it full of arrowroot
 And other necessary things,

And I will slay this fearful brute
With stones and sticks and guns and slings.

(A picture of

how people shoot

With comfort from a parachute.)

The Learned Fish

This learned Fish has not sufficient brains
To go into the water when it rains.

The Elephant

When people call this beast to mind,

They marvel more and more

At such a

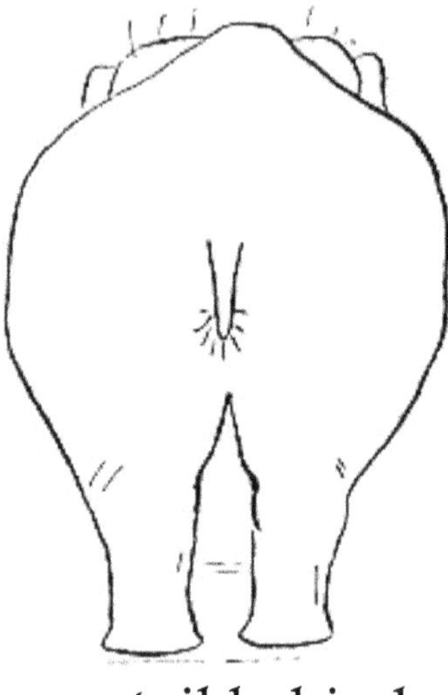

LITTLE tail behind,

So *LARGE* a trunk before.

The Big Baboon

The Big Baboon is found upon
    The plains of Cariboo:

He goes about

with nothing on

(A shocking thing to do).

But if he

dressed respectably

And let his whiskers grow,

How like this Big Baboon would be

To Mister So-and-so!

The Rhinoceros

Rhinoceros, your hide looks all undone,

You do not take my fancy in the least:

You have a horn where other brutes have
none:

Rhinoceros, you are an ugly beast.

The Frog

Be kind and tender to the Frog,

And do not call him names,
As 'Slimy skin,' or 'Polly-wog,'
Or likewise 'Ugly James,'
Or 'Gap-a-grin,' or 'Toad-gone-wrong,'
Or 'Bill Bandy-knees':

The Frog is justly sensitive
To epithets like these.

No animal will more repay
        A treatment kind and fair;
At least

                so lonely people say
Who keep a frog (and, by the way,
They are extremely rare).

Oh! My!

MORE BEASTS
(For WORSE CHILDREN)
VERSES BY H.B.
PICTURES BY B.T.B
ZOO

DEDICATION.

To

Miss ALICE WOLCOTT BRINLEY,

Of Philadelphia.

MORE BEASTS

FOR WORSE CHILDREN

INTRODUCTION

The parents of the learned child
        (His father and his mother)
Were utterly aghast to note
The facts he would at random quote
On creatures curious, rare and wild;
        And wondering, asked each other:

"An idle little child like this,
How is it that he knows
What years of close analysis
Are powerless to disclose?

Our brains are trained, our books are big,
And yet we always fail

To answer why the Guinea-pig
Is born without a tail.

Or why the Wanderoo* should rant
In wild, unmeaning rhymes,

*Sometimes called the "Lion-tailed or tufted Baboon of Ceylon."

Whereas the Indian Elephant
    Will only read *The Times.*

Perhaps he found a way to slip
Unnoticed to the Zoo,
And gave the Pachyderm a tip,
Or pumped the Wanderoo.

Or even by an artful plan
Deceived our watchful eyes,
And interviewed the Pelican,
Who is extremely wise."

"Oh! no," said he, in humble tone,
With shy but conscious look,
"Such facts I never could have known
But for this little book."

The Python

A Python I should not advise,—
It needs a doctor for its eyes,
And has the measles yearly.

However, if you feel inclined
To get one (to improve your mind,
And not from fashion merely),
Allow no music near its cage;

And when it flies into a rage
Chastise it, most severely.

I had an aunt in Yucatan
Who bought a Python from a man
    And kept it for a pet.
She died, because she never knew
These simple little rules and few;—

The Snake is living yet.

The Welsh Mutton

The Cambrian Welsh or Mountain Sheep
Is of the Ovine race,
His conversation is not deep,
But then—observe his face!

The Porcupine

What! would you slap the Porcupine?
Unhappy child—desist!
Alas! that any friend of mine
Should turn Tupto-philist.†

† From τυπτω=I strike; φιλεω=I love; one that loves to strike. The word is not found in classical Greek, nor does it occur among the writers of the Renaissance—nor anywhere else.

To strike the meanest and the least
    Of creatures is a sin,

How much more bad to beat a beast

With prickles on its skin.

The Scorpion

The Scorpion is as black as soot,
He dearly loves to bite;
He is a most unpleasant brute
To find in bed, at night.

The Crocodile

Whatever our faults, we can always engage
That no fancy or fable shall sully our page,
        So take note of what follows, I beg.
This creature so grand and august in its age,
        In its youth is hatched out of an egg.

And oft in some far Coptic town
The Missionary sits him down
    To breakfast by the Nile:
The heart beneath his priestly gown
    Is innocent of guile;

When suddenly the rigid frown
Of Panic is observed to drown
His customary smile.

Why does he start and leap amain,

And scour the sandy Libyan plain

Like one that wants to catch a train,

Or wrestles with internal pain?

Because he finds his egg contain—
Green, hungry, horrible and plain—
    An Infant Crocodile.

The Vulture

The Vulture eats between his meals,
And that's the reason why

He very, very rarely feels
As well as you and I.

His eye is dull, his head is bald,
His neck is growing thinner.
Oh! what a lesson for us all
To only eat at dinner!

The Bison

The Bison is vain, and (I write it with pain)
The Door-mat you see on his head

Is not, as some learned professors maintain,
The opulent growth of a genius' brain;

But is sewn on with needle and thread.

The Viper

Yet another great truth I record in my
verse,
That some Vipers are venomous, some the
reverse;
A fact you may prove if you try,

By procuring two Vipers, and letting them bite;

With the *first* you are only the worse for a fright,

But after the *second* you die.

The Llama

The Llama is a woolly sort of fleecy hairy
goat,
With an indolent expression and an
undulating throat
Like an unsuccessful literary man.

And I know the place he lives in (or at
least—I think I do)
It is Ecuador, Brazil or Chili—possibly
Peru;
You must find it in the Atlas if you can.

The Llama of the Pampasses you never
should confound
(In spite of a deceptive similarity of
sound)
With the Lhama who is Lord of Turkestan.

For the former is a beautiful and valuable
beast,
But the latter is not lovable nor useful in
the least;
And the Ruminant is preferable surely to
the Priest
Who battens on the woeful superstitions
of the East,
The Mongol of the Monastery of Shan.

The Chamois

The Chamois inhabits
Lucerne, where his habits
(Though why I have not an idea~r)

Give him sudden short spasms
On the brink of deep chasms,
And he lives in perpetual fear.

The Frozen Mammoth

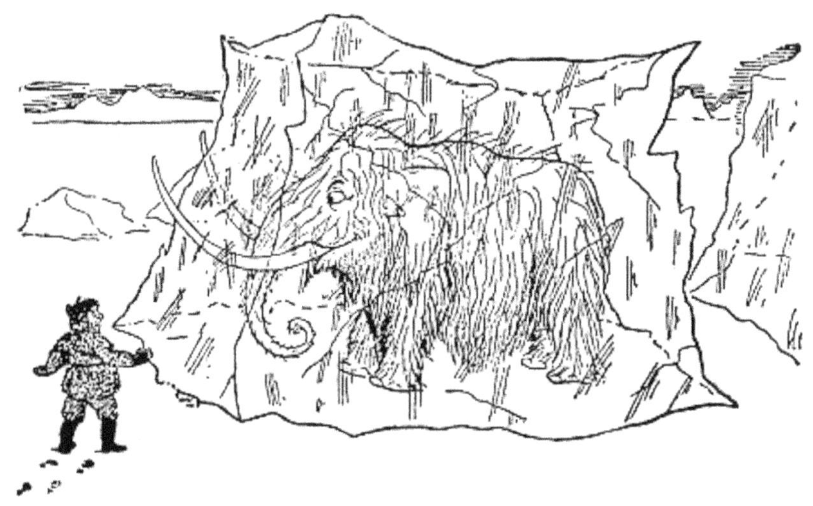

This Creature, though rare, is still found
to the East
Of the Northern Siberian Zone.

It is known to the whole of that primitive
group
That the carcass will furnish an excellent
soup,
Though the cooking it offers one
drawback at least
(Of a serious nature I own):

If the skin be *but punctured* before it is
boiled,
Your confection is wholly and utterly
spoiled.

And hence (on account of the size of the
beast)
The dainty is nearly unknown.

The Microbe

The Microbe is so very small
You cannot make him out at all,
But many sanguine people hope
To see him through a microscope.
His jointed tongue that lies beneath
A hundred curious rows of teeth;
His seven tufted tails with lots
Of lovely pink and purple spots,

On each of which a pattern stands,
Composed of forty separate bands;
His eyebrows of a tender green;
All these have never yet been seen—
But Scientists, who ought to know,
Assure us that they must be so. . . .
Oh! let us never, never doubt
What nobody is sure about!

Lightning Source UK Ltd.
Milton Keynes UK
UKHW011215091219
355041UK00003B/864/P